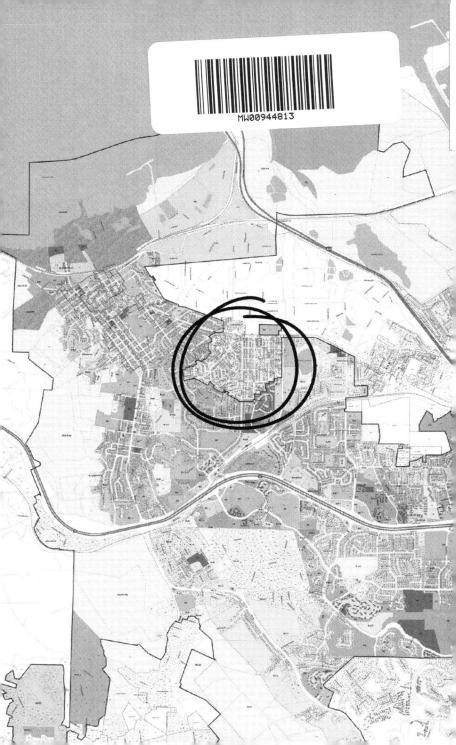

(s)words

contents

(s)words

(s)words

Cover by Daura Strassner
Contact: dstra.925@gmail.com

ISBN: 9781702804875

(s)words

for the kids
told they are too sharp

never fear your edges

use them

we the mud

pacheco

claims

spittle mouthed men hark cloud-ways as
do the souls they've fetched on fishing wire and
glinting lures.
they claim light , flowered mounds, pot-bellied
children,
i claim the tattered t-shirt dad wore,
the carquinez strait
and her industrial necklace,
the rust transferred to hands,
the truth in voices made silent,
in faces faded.

i trust in this will.
i know it claimed me.

weapons

(s)words bury
their serif bodies,
their soundless edges
into us,
to the hilt
to the bleeding ink handle.

like the weapons they are,
cutting the flesh of trees far less
than the pages of our scars,
tearing loose with every stroke and every stress
any tissue tightening these inflexible spines.

the thickest pages
with stories like muscle striating the lines,
don't cut so easy.
but skin that has not known pain,
nor the strong back of lineage,
is the easiest to break

(s)words are the only weapons
that have ever cut,
ever killed.

ask the murderer
to mop the blood from his mouth
with his crimson tie,
to better see
the razors in the vomit.

ask the murderer
to translate the screams

(s)words

of his messengers (bullets),
whose metal jackets
are filled with manifesto.

ask the murderer
if he cages light (humans)
so he can re-read
his given job description
in the monstrous shadow
of his own illness.

ask the murderer
if his weapon was given life
by the ones buried
in the soft belly
of his mind.

(s)words are the only weapons.

ask yourself,
do you wield them,
or do you wear them?

like an iron bouquet
in your chest.

i come from

i come from steel,
the marriage of alloys
against gods will,
carried in the veins of cemented
colonized marinas,
feeding machines far away
without asking if we are hungry.

i come from blood in the air,
blood on the coveralls, the shimmel,
blood on the sword and obsidian,
blood on the brain when it forgets
that i am from blood raw from scrubbing,
smudged with erasers and shadows.

i come from the birthwater,
the gunpowder banks of the rio grande,
the coarse fiber of mustache and desert brush.

i come from the atlantic and her mist.
i come from these handfuls of dirt,
the spores in our lungs,
and the next paycheck for purchasing air.

i come from the carport's bent beam,
the seas of ivy between our cells.
i come from wheels and their speed,
the miles racked up circling the same block.

i come from tragedy,
and tragic assumptions.
i come from tampico and otter pops,

and the sting at our mouth's corners.

i come from the bottom of the bottle
and an ocean of their skeletons,
ready to be topped off and sealed for
special occasions or the grave.
i come from poets who belong in fistfights,
in the testing grounds behind fosters,
inside the vice of pubescent muscle.

i come from prismed legacy,
from dreams pruned to the trunk,
from smoke,
and security in circles
in a town rotating counterclockwise.

i come from hangnails
and the aging redwood responsible.
i come from duct tape adorning
the framing hammer's collarbone,
from tv dinners and the lunchbox dad sat on
to watch us scrape the plastic clean.
i come from the plastic crack of heads
before the meal.
from my mother's silent promise
to give us more than she could give.

i come from the library book on school steps,
i come from screw and scalpel tattoos,
from the 5-minute poem,
from the apparition i was at every open mic
i attended in secret,
i come from the thickest welds in these lungs,
from this stainless steel, cooling tower trachea
which breathes fire

(s)words

despite its origin,
despite the soil and stick walls
of 2 atriums,
2 ventricles,
1 tree trunk aorta.

i come from this balance
the both here and there
the disgraced ore and it's mother

i come from this curse
from knowing both must exist,
from knowing i am not stainless,
from knowing these (s)words
are forever stronger
than any steel in me.

steel

we wanted it to be disneyland

157,000 barrels a day
are pumped from (us) these ivory towers,
this chain-smoking skyline
opposite pacheco blvd.

the siren,
the klaxon whining like bomb raid
every first wednesday
sent us scattering like mice,
pretending the end had come
and it wasn't only a test.

our only view was this oil refinery,
on burning summer afternoons,
on the hill behind the complex,
from the single pane window,
near the bunk beds.
we thought it was disneyland,
with its firelight and magic rust.

can we go there mom?

what it pumped from us those days was fuel.
the willingness to get beyond its eyes.
the strength to be more than our father's replica.
because here,
that is what we all were.
vessels of tradition,
one-dimensional manhood,
and smoke rising
from fires

(s)words

not expected to last.

here,
opposite pacheco blvd,
our neighbors sleepy from the night shift
working in its iron guts,
we became the tiny blood cells
in the capillaries
of industrial cardiac tissue,
pumping,
cyclical,
like machinery,
the theme park sound system on loop.

spinning like fumes from the smokestacks,
and seeing only closest turn,
or next hit,
or the next chance to grumble
how we should've won state,
how 157,000 barrels can escape
but we can't, or didn't, or won't.

we are the unremembered
who remember our place too well,
on the other side of pacheco,

unsure if the view is magic,
or magic trick.

american receipts

the people without,
who suffered the trans(action) of this plunder,
have had these very american receipts
folded under fingernails,
and have read the fine print.

return the damned souls of
columbus, alvarado, pizarro as collateral
for the cremated and desecrated.
return the silver arteries and golden bowels
of postosí, of minas gerais,
zacatecas and guanajuato.
return the indian backs you broke
because cattle were too expensive.
return the burning entrails of veracruz children
to their bodies so they might reingest the blood of
cortes.

expedite
the english and the dutch and the french
to the final pulpit,
to brand their triangular trade,
their holy trinity,
into their sickly,
silver skin.

return the african hearts you drowned
and disembodied in caribbean seas,
on west african shores.
the oceans rise now in revolution,
as did(do) the ones who survived.

(s)words

return the flayed feet and severed heads
of campesinos turned guerrilleros,
made immortal by their martyrdom.
stich back together their rich bodies
so they may walk in flesh
and spirit before young, dark eyes.

return the 10,000 free souls of palmares,
the longest slave rebellion in history,
who were cut down
in your crusade for capital gain.
return the 3,900 pairs of african ears
from the saddle bags of portuguese captains,
so they may hear the feet of their children,
still here,
still amassing in dark corners,
inevitable through time,
like overgrowth in your abandoned latifundias,
ransacked because they were never rooted.

return your manufactured paranoia.
your manichean measures spin tales of goodness,
but not of thievery,
speak of horror like it was holistic,
instead of human,
says you are civilized,
instead of savage.

return the bulging fats
cut from the yellow bellies
of your european banks,
which gorged on this land.

return your greed,
the receipts are these hands,

printed onto the helixes
of the earth-colored bones
in every human being
still breaking on your wheel.

return your ignorance,
you stand tall on these bloody volumes,
your soft feet keep these covers pinned.

return your malice,
your evil is measured in your soulless money,
in the breaths stolen from the crackling lungs
of the indios you made siphon it at gunpoint.

return to what you owe,
because while you may escape
again and again
to another virgin land,
your silver hands are stained red
like two blood moons in the dark,
and all will know:
that the oceans refused to cleanse you,
the forests refused to feed you,
because you refused to see(d) them.

your hands will be buried into the horizon,
and cut away so you cannot dig them out,
obliging your 500-year preference
to
feel
nothing.

all will know,
you will never escape these scales,

(s)words

now held
not by your silver hands,
but by the ones you cut away,
that you did not know
were receipts,
and
seeds.

when a man opens his hand

men have cleaved open this world,
shattering more than shielding,
splitting instead of sewing (sowing).

every time
a man unfolds the
crumpled poem of his fist,
he creates a negative space,
a hollow in his palm
in which worlds can be created and held,
in which another's hand can rest
and leave warmer than before,
in which the embryos of better men
have room to stretch.

when a man opens his hand
he may sample the infinity of a woman,
his own origin,
his hand becomes the inverse,
a place to hold life's pencil,
to leave a mark, for once
that is not a scar.

the tender palm laid bare.
the flower bed in concrete.

every bleeding knuckle embellishing
the false crown of this fist,
this phallic sledgehammer,
will testify:
these hands were never meant
to close and break.

they are birthed
in Gods(her) grace,
they are birthed,
to open,
to hold,
to birth again.

balance

white people: a prognosis

to whom it may concern,

there are ten bullets filed
into the death beds of magazines,
for every one "conversation"
you have about this sickness.

no disease has ever been drawn out
with discussion,
yet you presume to think
you will gallantly cure this pestilence
you wrote into the hems of blankets
and shipdecks.

if your death depended on it (your life does),
conversation would be out.

if your blood pressure was a pendulum
every time you clocked-in to life,
like it is for so many,
you would choose to seize
instead of "analyze" its long swing.

ironically,
white blood cells sprint through arteries
to mend any holes,
to fight any sickness in the flesh.

and in the expanse of all time,
not a single white blood cell
had a conversation,
or pretended to not know,

(s)words

or scoffed at poems like this,
before it hurried,
and moved.

so hurry up.

move.

we the mud

i feel like wet dirt,
soil being smashed into a fax machine,
like i must be translated into an electrical signal
so people receive me better,
like the truth we stand on
is better understood from photographs with a
caption
than if it were beneath our own feet.

i contend the beat of this song, the heat of this
unrest, right now, in this chest,
in this moment,
is better than the copy wrung from its body.
how can i love you if i do not feel you?
and instead attempt only to translate,
with words that do not exist
in your hearts mother tongue.
how can i love you if i do not feel you,
how can i love you if i do not feel you,
how can i rise up with you
if i do not hear you?
i will not codify what you are
because you, like me, and they and she
are infinite scrolls
of pain and seethe and heartbreak and dreams,
which cannot conform to 1s and 0s.

yet still you divide the soul of my words
into digestible dichotomy,
like you can see no God in me,
like you are columbus on the shores
of a soon-to-be raped land
assigning meaning, applying reason

and science to the beat-beating sounds
of beautiful hearts,
with no regard for why they were made at all,
do not forget that
the cross-bearing crusader,
conquistador,
and classroom teacher
can all cut throats in the same way,
and finger-paint disparities for display
in some room
where everything will be said,
but nothing will be done.
all this earth-colored skin
split with covered ears,
you forget the heads you put on spears,
you forget to rear your children to remember,
you say death in the ears
of the dismembered bodies
that feed your machines.
how can you digitize lungs into to-do list and d-
dashes when the flesh they are made of is muraled
with gashes,
this is for every diatribe colonized
with calls for "civility",
for every heart-scream silenced
in the name of "decorum",
and for every truth cut down
by "decency",
for every betrayal framed
as "business",
and for every post-partum sob painted
as "progress".

how do you heal half a nation
from stockholm syndrome?

(s)words

especially when the serial killer's white skin is
government issue and tagged normal
and "not the issue",
the given costume custom fit to
see no evil,
hear no evil,
speak no evil,
lethal,
lethal,
lethal,
for every program the cost is people,
for every coded logarithm
the profit is hijacked cardiac rhythm
they speak to me like keyboards
and click-click into my chest
to commandeer this heart,

this handful of wet earth,

and tell it to fit in the spread sheet,
because otherwise it won't make sense,
it doesn't feed the GDP when it's bleeding stories
instead of dollars and cents,
this heart is made from mud,
and the blood of ancestors blended,
staining these descending white collars
like collectors of the dead and downloaded,
like the tie-wearing reapers
of the human being they are
slinging pistols and swinging scantron sickles
at these sensations.
i am tired of being too much to translate,
of being reduced to d-data,
i wear caverns in this skin
as signifiers of the sand displaced,

(s)words

of the land erased,
of the hands defacing stories with censorship
and pages ripped out
leaving no place for this love to go,
this love i know, this truth i show is
all that holds me together.
this bond between protons and planets,
and palms in prayer,
and people anywhere cannot be severed,
cannot be sifted from blood that rushes
unexplainably to these throats when truth
is sped into the songs of our voices,
do not tell me to switch nicely
like circuit breaker,
to make slideshows and
easy to swallow soundbytes
of these symphonies,
because every muddy cell has a story to tell,
because we are here to speak,
and to love,
and to connect to what's above,
to speak the stories you're afraid of,

we are the mud,
we are the mud,
we are the mud,

and we are your salvation,
there is no equation to make us more patient,
listen to these ancients,
or expect repayment,
data will never cure your ailment.
it will forever be this mud,

and the decay of your slave ships,

(s)words

and the decay of your slave chips,

your microchips,

i dare you,
translate this.

marina

press play

device in hand,
the edges machined smooth.
press play.
press your cheek the other way, like always,
so you might forget whose names hinge on
hashtags,
the ones cold beyond ticker tape,
and safely floating in your living room,
leaking, losing letters in the static
because the screens bear fruit each second of each
day,
google search to google search,
flashes to flashes,
dust to dust,
to dead.
but it is not your son.
nor anyone you knew with dreams and 4 heart
valves,
he was not your son.
just the 9pm newsspeak hum
of anchors dislodging minds and turning tales
in the empty space.
those bullet points, fact sheets, shot through the
trigger of your mouse click or iphone flick or
statistics claiming there is no fault,
nor stick of injustice on the side of power,
the side of power,
the lies of power,
device in hand,
device (uncle sam),
device in hand,
device (white man),
device in hand,

33

(s)words

device (i am)
standing between power and titillation,
between power and indoctrination,
between power and a well-trained nation,
emancipation proclamation a commiseration,
all sensation, your brown brothers?
no relation.
we need freedom now?
don't fit the equation,
this game been yours but education blows the
budget,
information injurious to the money pit,
plus the dewy eyes of your white child
couldn't bear to know the wicked,
the slick and crimson hands of white men
bearing whips, white skin, and the predisposition
to habit.
america is careful to not offend you, not to upend
you,
to contend the status quo,
because dead bodies stay sensations,
soothsayers of the screen to the safe and drowning,
the nilla wafer crowning dialect of men with
micro megaphones, blaring into homes which vile
to load,
which vein to stick so the venom works best,
be careful to not forget white faces
prefer humans not as souls,
but as soundwaves,
as gigabytes, not white,
be careful to keep having,
to keep jabbing your credit cards into things
we wish to own,
into things you still wished you owned,
never mind the bones,

the centuries of shackles and spoon fed,
songs of women red and men sped to the heaviest
gavel,
who escaped the transaction,
but still pay with lives every second of every day,
with fear,
with the young mind which can't see a way out
because nobody else can either,
it is time to recognize that the ancestors of your
armchair architects are in your finger everyday
pressing play,
because these human beings are made to be make
believe,
because to you, to me, they are meant to scream
through computer screens:

"all according to plan"

device in hand,
device (i am),
these edges machined smooth,
like the bullets that will never tear down
the door of your breastbones,
device (white man),
device (uncle sam),
device (i am),
go ahead,
do nothing,
but press play.

parenthetical

we (understand the explosion and colors,
but not the chemical reaction in the lungs
of the rocket holding its breath.

we understand the bloody nose and broken hand,
but not the electricity chambering an elbow.

we understand the slurs and condescension,
but not the crucible broiling stimuli in their hearts.

we understand the poem,
but not the spark stringing together chaos in our
souls,
to sling open its womb.

we understand the parenthetical,
but can't, for the life of us, employ it when we
speak,
even though so many words
need libraries between their letters.

we understand the creation,
but not the limbo of formation.

these silver tongues
speak darkness as evil,
and have the world convinced.
but it is in darkness we are made,
in darkness we dream,
in darkness new life is curled,
in darkness the roots reach,
in darkness there is magic,

(s)words

that evil bedfellow for anything
(white) science cannot explain.

if darkness is wrong,
why is every day balanced by darkness and her
stars,
mapping our way home?

what if this limbo,
this soil, this space between,
the impossible, invisible parenthetical,
that this language won't allow

is God

shutting off the light,
so that our eyes, as intended,
are useless in the shadow of our dreams.
so that new life, as intended, may) rise.

(s)words

arana

authorship

when we hear the word
author
we often think of the being with
half their soul in the typewriter,
or acclaimed by some authority
that is never our own.
we find comfort in authors who write ink on paper,
who tattoo the earth in preservation,
who may even by chance,
write a shadow of ourselves in the binding.

it hit me one day
after sheetrocking the basement with my dad,
and talking authenticity with my mother,
that they are the greatest authors
i have ever known.

my parents labored behind their hands
for 24+19 years,
to write my brother and i.
with crossed fingers and sweat,
with hope in nothing but the next page,
their shitty handwriting urgently penned,
made room for us to interpret the symbols.

what volume is more acclaimed by God,
than our own bodies,
filled to the teeth with memory?

what story is more worthy of celebration,
than the one that refuses to end,
because you are still here?

which authors deserve immortality more
than the ones who have survived the fires?

my dna is one endless parable,
authored by women
who tell stories with their faces,
replicated in my own,
bound by the leather embrace of hands
that did not have the courage to write
until they became mine.

these false prophets of our world,
this contradiction of a society
says real authors write.

i say real authors
survive long enough
to see their stories live.

"we interrupt this marriage to bring you the
football season"

wealth

to the kids who never had sleepovers
at their house,
because that shit was too small,
too under-construction,
because mom could use the break.

to the kids who got told next christmas
there will be presents,
but this year we got each other,
who never got into cabinets without asking,
who came from cycles
of not having access or excess,
or currency for milk,
or clothes,
or love.

our gift was the understanding
that the poorest among us
have the fruit,
but no respect for the labor of it's seed.

our gifts are the trowels at the ends our wrists,
and the plows nailed to our feet.

our gift is a respect for the rain,
the mud,
and the neighbors plot.

we are the wealth
intended by God.
the kind that takes wing and roots
miles beyond the high fences.

to feed more than
your friend's big-ass house
ever could.

wounded lions

bloody, grown
the broken high grass
reaches still,
by and by the body,
around it, surround it,
orange drips and puddles
wafting warmth on a dusted crust
cloaked scarlet now,
for this is the latter half-light,
where the king resides collar
sponged dark, alone, save what
flora persists to cradle his crown
thatched and gold,
in this failing flame,
a fire now whipped and pensive,
cascading the coals of erstwhile time
upon his sweetest dreams,
over the clout of a glinting spirit,
and even in this,
in the telltale hour
as the winds kneel,
his bellow is heard,
his aura is flexed,
bowing out,
fit to offend his fall
because he hasn't,
never will,
wont,
cant,
while his eyes shimmers still,
while his heart's throb wafts ever stronger
than the fading scarlet light.

smolder

midway through august, 1962.
a little boy was born to parents that
had love enough for ten more.
they named him michael and gave him ten
helpings,
every day until his eyes loosened into spyglasses
filled with sky.
he was fire.

so much so that one night
he dreamt himself into sun,
into 620 million metric tons of maybes on wings,
his skin crackled, his blood humming white hot
into his pillow, an applause by every red cell he
had but,
he never heard it coming.

*"ma'am your son is deaf. for as long as he lives
he will require powerful listening aids to
communicate. he will struggle with speech and
will be severely disadvantaged in the school
environment. ma'am your son will be different."*

your son will be different,
different,
the words rifled through
the barrel of some md's mouth
and mushroomed,
like lead roses in a garden that too will die,
but still has its moments,
every pedal cutting its way into bloom.

(s)words

but soon they would know,
that michael couldn't hear the gunshots anyway,
and so he grew,
with different dangling from his jaw,
tucked away wires,
and an earpiece tuned into whatever God was,
be it the mighty thor
or slurpees after swim practice,
and damn did he listen,
to every vibration and whistle,
to every left-side heavy swivel of his lips,
every homing-missile carrying words
like "dumb" or "deafling",
which always hit their mark
but somehow missed that heart of his,
every part of him had u-turns
for any asshole with a mouth,
for any jackals with clout enough to pester
a 90-pound freshman itching to hit the gym,
their mouths, id bet, still taste like fist
and first-team all-league,
michael never stopped burning you see.

he could never hide the bullseye that vaporized
anything near it. the kid had spirit to spare,
that flared out in mile-wide ribbons of flame,
and charged the atmosphere
of each person he met,
even himself, when he flickered on instinct
he would ask my grandfather tough questions.

"dad. why can't i be a fireman,
dad, why can't i be a pilot or an astronaut,
why did my 6th grade english teacher spear me
with an f-,

(s)words

is it because i can't hear them,
is it because i talk funny,
is it because i'm broken,
because i'm different?"

yes michael,
because the tarmac would boil,
because the stars would want you back,
and because some people prefer carbon copies,
i couldn't tell you how he spoke, my grandfather.
nor how he slept knowing that my father, michael,
would have one less thing
to dream about that night,
his different ignited reality on every shadow
thrown by nightlights, but different had triggers
on every light switch,
hairpinned and primed for sunshine
and shiny-new hearing aid batteries,
different was not him, because he wears it,
proudly,
dominoed in the firework wrinkles on his face
that he got from one smile too many,
he wears it, like i wear him in my words,
in my far overgrown pilot light,
he wears it in every name
he might stumble over or mispronounce,
and i swear to God that no amount of
"nevermind" or *"what did you say?"*
could stop him from listening,
from scorching different
into the pinewood of his hands,
from bringing both to me and
boughing happiness from my shoulder saying

"listen…could you hear that?

(s)words

in the wind, that different,
like your voice, does not sway,
it belongs to you, so wear it, son,
stitch it to your lips and do some smiling today,
wish it nowhere else
but the treeknots in your palms
and the embers in your heart, grow it stark from
every inch of skin you own
like wires rooted to your chest, and
synapse until something sounds familiar,
and when it finally does tell
the ones who don't like it
to dial in elsewhere or kindly fuck off,
because if the sun goes out
all you'll have left is you,
and you better hope you like that guy,
you better hope your light rips at the sky
long enough
to light a fire beneath somebody else,
i need you to smolder, son,
to glow boldly where dullness
swindled real estate
on your spyglass eyeballs,
to gleam like i knew you had to,
i need you to promise me,
that misconceptions will come second
to stargathering, stargazing was
never my thing either,
there is different rising
through your wishing-well pores,
like buckets and buckets of good fortune
fasten it strong, this smile,
with pride in your teeth,
with the words that i let by.

(s)words

go on and burn now.
because i know,
that midway through june, 1992,
a little boy was born to parents
that had love enough for ten more.

and he was fire.

oceans

i never knew what pain was for
until i waded into it with gentle hands,
before it receded.

in my short life,
pain has tried to soak in between the splits of this
skin,
tried to flood my foundations into swamps.

but i've made alarm clocks of its warning bells,
made sentences of its sear and swell,
made the frothing crescendo of its orchestra
a prayer in my body.

pain has be(come)
the only ocean i do not fear.

carquinez

but i bled

he's just like my father.
(deadbeat)(absent)(unhealed)(drunk)

i was never meant to hear it,
this bandolier belt of a sentence
strapped to my mother's tongue.
this ticking vest, for which there was no key.

bullets tear no flesh just lying on the table.
grenades shatter no air resting in the fruit bowl.
knives sever nothing with no hand to say
here.

i was never meant to hear it.
but i bled,
and bled,
and
bled

circles

your arms full circle around me,
the shape you've paced in while saving my life,
the shape of cycles you could not escape,
the attempted shape at a poem
to make it make sense,
spiraling lower,
but not connecting in the storm.

it took me 27 rotations
to see that like mine,
your love is a hurricane.

its beautiful pirouette misunderstood
by any linear line of sight,
which can see the spin,
but not feel its physics.

you, mom,
are a hurricane.
who let us into the stillness of your eye,
who, after the storm, showed us
how to see what really matters.

your love will forever remind me
to fear not of man,
but of you and your kind of righteous embrace.
to love not delicately,
but forcefully, powerful,
through the spume,
because this is the only way
to distinguish weeds from the deeply rooted.

(s)words

they will never understand your dance.
they won't look past forecast to see
that with your strength
you have eddied my own soul into a storm.

they will never understand
that you have been though every kind of rain,
to better learn its language,
so you could teach it to us,
so we are never left guessing when it falls.

they choose never to understand,
that beyond the muscle of your swells,
the force of your nature,

there is love.
raging to be felt.
raging,
to come full circle.

chariots

they rode me in on chariots.
there were banners on the wind,
rust in my nailbeds i remember.
the kneeling grass and alabaster breath-woven
death of day
chasing west, to send me home.
i'm sure it was manhood.

these hands should know it they said
when other 'men' say
they've sewn it into overcoats
and into one or two-word tragedies,
their chronicles waving from two
one-way windowpanes
set on necks made from dying trees
those men spoke with sinew.

with the news that bone will grow dense
and impossible,
i have seen us try, for the right and high kind of
sweat, the kind we let sizzle into lesson
within the fire of friday nights,
we were tailless kites set free towards the sun,
the sons of men who had no war but
wished us soldiers
so we did not die,
except in pieces.

so in the creases of our wounds
we left them for a day
when pain was alright with us,
when humility rode shotgun

(s)words

and compassion had the wheel,
but most of us couldn't drive yet, you see
we were visions of men,

riding a gauntlet grown old,
the one of glory and giftedly broken skins,
that leak scarlet and searing red stories from
knuckles that sometimes
just want another's to lock with,
but our locksmith had gone fishing,
because those you can throw back,
they wont stain your face or make you a pussy,
so we fished,

we sat and wished
that beer bottles carried away our cries
to people that gave two shits, because somehow
an sos was better left unwritten.
better stored or spilt into endorphin,
into grinding teeth
or the siege of flooded body,
our blood would snap into neurons,
i speak of manhood that is measured in scars,
in barbells and one-nightstands
the men that howled past my chariot in 69
mustangs,
was i,
was i enough.

was i the stuff of story books.
would i be the man that shook history by its toes
until change fell from its pockets,
would i drawl with wisdom or tear down tyranny,
walk with spacemen or win super bowl 50,
save the planet, get the girl,

(s)words

nobody said i had to do these things,

but what boy doesn't aspire
to himself late at night,
wanting the world to know him,
or maybe just that girl to notice him
and some, brave enough to need it, just want a
chance to meet love, to shake its hand then to
dance inside and not feel indecent or weak when
the forgotten but indigenous speak of soul crashes
through their eardrums,
i was the one,
who felt it strumming the strings
of my too-eager instrument,
who felt butterfly atom bombs in my gut but said
nothing
because the other men may tell me too much,
too much for a boy to say follow me,
when he rides nothing but a splintering chariot.

but now i carry it closer
to the legends that some men lived,
now coded with the pieces they left into catacomb
or the scripture of my long bones,
pieces not within the creases of wounds
nor cleft of chin,
but within the breast of men
strong enough to feel something,
i will remember,
that even though the torrents of their hearts,
though the vigor of their cells did expire,
their integrities did not,
i have heard that real men never but cry,
but then i remember that real men never die,
they are alive in me, in every tear

(s)words

or bead of sweat that i've spent,
within every ascension, or mention of greatness
or trembling
beat,
beat,
there are men trenched deep with shields,
and one day when my wheels
draw near ill know them,
i'll show to them my scars and they'll say

no,
show me your heart.

show me the muscle
that never felt your dumbbells and mirror,
and now tell me,
what do you see?

when you breathe does it too?
is it wreathed with your truth?
with your love's hue is it beaming?
does it know the meaning of your dreams?

i dreamed last night of chariots
but woke up before i got there.
i sat up in my bed to find the hide
of my hand still solid,
to find the concussions in my chest
like two hammers
speaking love poems as if morse code
was their birth-given tongue,
i am not the one with muscle car.

so if you were to ask me
if knew what it meant to be a man,

(s)words

i couldn't say
but, without question,
i could tell you where to look.

dogs

mechanic

every nerve that jettisoned an sos
into the sky of my mind to make me feel pain,
i am grateful for.

because with every primitive message
screaming like a red-lining engine
on this highway of scars still under construction,
i got a closer look under the hood.

i l(earned) how the tiny explosions
chugged in succession,
in rhythms,
like the first human being to beat a drum
on the skin of an animal who exploded the same.

i am grateful
because i have become
the mechanic of my own suffering.

a pyrotechnician
calculating the explosions,
tinkering with the rhythms
in this rust.

love to the lost

to every kid who ever doodles trancelike in the
first 10 minutes of class or tears paper into tiny
confetti for the celebration of nothing but another
day or builds gravity-defying towers of
condiments with artful mastery at the diner dinner
table or creates entire worlds and planets in the
corners of school notebooks or makes sound
effects when they pretend-fight friends who are
too lame to make sounds back or cross-dresses in
the talent show with their mom's clothes because
their magician friend can't not have a lovely
assistant or talks to their toys kindly before bed in
case they suddenly have murderous urges in the
night or gives up God spitefully after part of them
dies or goes to sleep in their 8:45 class every day
because they're fucking tired or cries specifically
in the shower or leaves at 3am to walk aimlessly
and talk to spiders in the dark or has a heart like a
tesla coil and gets called crazy even though they
know the secret to free energy or knows for certain
the tsa "randomly searched" their bag on purpose
or wonders how shitty people sleep at night or
done anything remotely similar to things in this list
or found out God never gave them up or makes art
out of books and music and time and 5 gum
wrappers and time and love and pain and wonder
and park benches and passive aggressive adults
and nothing and nothing and nothing and turns it
into something

beautiful.

(s)words

i feel you.
and if you keep losing the map, like always,
someone else will put equally lost hands on you in
the dark,
and you won't be alone.
i promise.

kid

(s)words

(s)words whisper in their sheaths,
rattle metallic warning,
these steel snakes on our lips,
coiled and humming
the sting of kinetic energy,
louder, louder.

these words are carried to kill nothing
but the hand that reaches too close,
these words are protecting
a sacred equilibrium,
one their unequal hearts intend to upset,
they will claim it was gravity's fault,
louder,
louder,

these (s)words are the vanguard
of new life birthed.

mother's fangs keeping back the buzzards.

the cause's effect.

the venom guaranteed.

in the tireless defense of balance
between the odds,
and the only things worth protecting.

louder,
louder,
they rattle always.

blossom

your roots
split the earth,
jostle in their conformation.
between sandstone and sod,
they drink.
i have placed my hands
about your waist, and felt life
then for the first time, what
swelling my cells were warmed to.
by translation
i quaver, by the very nature of your skin.
but sitting beneath your hardy limbs,
i would not have known.
that the snows have chilled your pulp,
that the sun has blistered your ambling boughs,
that you were inhabited, by ghosts,
and might.
and the latter i do know,
because in stunning revolt,
your roots have procured a blossom
that has yet to die.

famine

spent like
famine bread.
my eyes glaze at the hour.
the sun is halfway tucked beneath
this valley's muscular back.
another day, worn in with certitude's thumb.
maple leaves have their glow,
the din of a drowsy city is still tolerable.
happiness walks me home,
then tonight ill flop onto my bed and think of your
laugh.

and for some odd reason,
i keep finding crumbs in my pocket.

love

caught in the spaces between rooftops,
calamity has lassoed the moon
and brought it close,
its slicing glow, evermore a mason.
there is absence in my defense,
a departure for the sake of some underthought
that might boil and rise, where
again at the bloody heels of tides and sand,
i decidedly do nothing—feeling onward in the
dark,
by gusty incentive.
by reason and hope.
kneading with my thoughts the dampness of 2am.
why it is damp, and where it places things.
why when subject to its wisdom it is me, but i am
not it.
and why i would bother leaving this temple.
this absurd, little bench.

i have one guess.

belong here

another absence,
wrung by revelation, by
the motions of weekends
and terribly late monday nights
that have groaned
themselves together.
momentum is a powerful thing.
but not perpetual,
not like memory, or names.
i find myself sputtering out, desperate words,
parts of me,
beside that broken lawn chair on the porch,
with the stresses and falling-outs of phrases like
"i don't give a fuck".
a part of me left here and there,
wandering the veins of a city
kept by names.
levied by momentous ambitions,
the naivete of my ribs
rippling names through my head
whenever i wonder:
will my name belong here?

fool

he wants nothing more than nothing,
wants thrumming noontime, empty skin,
clear of misfired nerves.
the days have spooled in his gut, so many,
never met, because another reel toils over in his
chest
like a factory machine left for weeds,
or vagrant truth.

tired, of drowsing for weeks,
of guilt squatting in his bones.

so trivial, it seems, exhausted to
each pen stroke, to every sense that committed
treason,
to the well-spoken sunrise.

but even so,
a few hours before dawn, some nights, he nails
back his
eyelids with every other thought,
too fearful of dreams.
he's nothing,
but a damn fool.

fragile

our hearts are fragile on purpose.

the ones that pump the hardest
have been completely destroyed,
and rebuilt,
and rebuilt,
and (re)built.

to withstand the heat,
to withstand hammers waiting in line
to try us out
on purpose.

claws

for naked land,
these cedar and fir,
autumn stirs, from the apex of shadows long.
conversations between this southern-most fork
are mortal.
their nebulous bellies,
their roots and flesh will
grow down
into sky.
a lone fox lingers by its bank, wanting
to grow somewhere that is not his wood,
he had once bounded through
with young reverie, and wagging tongue.
he is eyed, by an autumn newly chilled,

his wood has grown claws.

rummaging

i stole an apple, 2 bottles from the can.

tecate, bud light, pisswater.

i stole them because my throat scratched.

the beer was gone and not for me.

the apple was for my shirt sleeve.

this carboard sign is for me.

anything helps.

the ganglia of too many fears.

dislodging and firing.

squad upon beggar.

aim for the heart.

bush plane

forgive me, the stammer in my shoes,
this moth wing pulse, suggesting cadence
for the propeller, or for the pendulums
in my sentences, for how they swing into you
then back because gravity wont reconsider.
the wright brothers, somewhere between
a running start and the cosmos,
could understand.

i remember that i've always been a bush plane.
pitching wildly through heart valves,
vena cava and canyon, the rising conifer breath
with my own, braiding skyward,
where i may struggle
to find you.

however gorgeous, the trees again remind me.
that with their flesh and the nerve of two people,
gravity was no more.

face

to reach in this way,
in this manner, unlike forceps and their words
is always written.
made accessible in your eyes.
tracing me,
the un-technical poem,
a drop in the river,
in colors i do not wish to know.
there is often writing of smiles.
but in yours there in no device.
only me, and this minute.
what we write into tremors
beneath our necks.

fruit

we did not forecast pain.
but to focus on it,
to constrict irises to find it,
is to give it sun and stream,
to flood the irrigated claw marks of the heart.

pain can weep, grow, transform
into flowers.
into fruit.

hands

we hold them now.
hands that steal away
for the fear of being authentic.
gimbaled over wrists that reveal it anyway.
what we need fizzling
in the estuary of nerve endings
fingertip, tuning fork,
the administrative end
to feeling happiness holding phones,
waiting to move, to pick up and speak differently,
to ramble in the flash-hems and nuances
a thread or naval rope of you,
lasting moments, one phone call,
the tender underbelly of palms given up
to pens or clicking keys, if not,
God willing,
another hand turned in chance.

peace

we will pain our fingers to find it.
flutter through p(s)alms,
home-remedy sermons,
like a hand through tall grass,
trying to soar into the remaining daylight.

we singe the door handles into peace
because we fear it will lock behind us,
and then what are we without the daggers
we keep like baby teeth,
which hurt so much.

what else can we be but our suffering born again,
stored in matchboxes?

we are the earthquake in our own foundations,
the impulse to keep turning in the fields,
the matchstick and scripture,
cut from the same tree,
aching to ignite.

origin

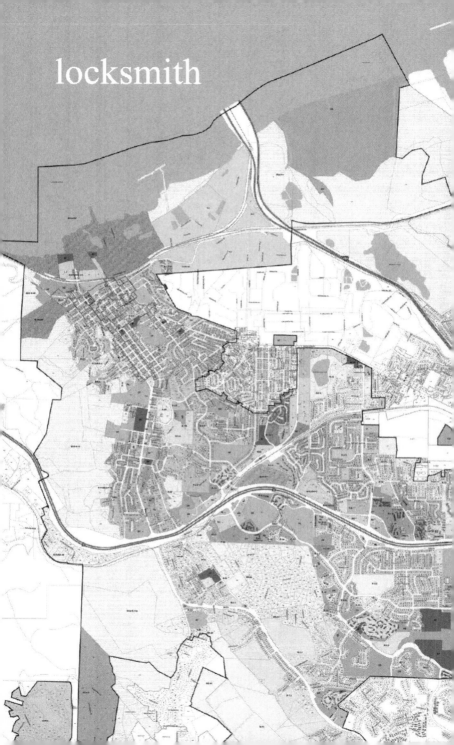

the first day of poetry

you know, last night,
on the eve of explaining something so explosive,
so human and unintentional as poetry,
i was wordless.
i couldn't muster the language needed
to tell my students
that a poem is not a poem at all,
no.

a poem is not words on a page,
nor the sage upon stage,
nor the fuming rage of pages ripped and aged,
not caged in the antiseptic mazes
of hoity-toity academic stages
for getting a's and stuff,
for getting grades and praise and stuff,
for dazing otherwise beautiful brains
and stuff.

no, on the eve of my explaining
to a room full of kids
that they should need a poem i was not wordless
because i didn't know,
but because i tried to know to know too much,

a poem is brainless baby, smooth and free-flow,
grooved and beat-go, pbbt and easy-go go go
crazy,
the pick-apart ploys of teachers forgetting
are not on the menu,
this is a buffet for the gods,
but more for the moments they envy us,
the mortal morsels of time

(s)words

spitting and slinging flames
without an ounce of magic in their bones,
the poems we write are homes
for the groaning ache to feel something,
to be somebody,
to seethe and cry and beat our chests
not because we want to,
but because we need to,
because we breathe to be alive,
not to die day-by-day in the carcass of being
comfortable,
conform-aton,
fill-in-the-bubble-and-fall-in-line-a-thon
on every station and crooked communication
communicated for indoctrination to a nation
not intended to be,
we need vibrations.
we were never meant to rot, or blot wounds,
to block or clot tunes that come out of us,
the poem is the spigot we need to turn,
the burns we gotta bare to all
because our scars are the most gorgeous braille
this earth gives us,
the poem will be our bane and our heartbeat
in the same second,
it will inject sweet relief and turn the knife
in our guts like a top,

but,

the poem never leaves.
the poems, like worn-out keys,
jangle in our pockets everyday
waiting for the right door.

(s)words

the poem is our savior,
our bike ride at 3am,
our run-away from home,
the song that gives like christmas,
the words you would never say,
the tears we cannot catch with our shirt sleeve,
the "i love you mom no matter what",
the need to say i'm good enough for love,
i'm good enough to be loved,
the anger steaming in your ribs,
the middle finger you want to give everybody in
the room,
the day after your world crumbles,
and the smile you put on anyway
all in the same moment

you see the poem can't possibly be explained.
so,
let me show you.

ruffling feathers

best to not ruffle feathers
you told me.
best to stay low.
do what you're told.
fly this formation
(until it's all you know).

praise to the highest
that i could not listen.

this goes out to every grown human being
who, against flock, gave the finger,
because this is how every good thing starts,
as an act of flight
in the opposite direction.

to every teacher
who retraced their course with stars
instead of state mandates.

to every silenced, soil-skinned youth,
who despite the ultimate risk,
followed their hearts
instead of rules.

i sing their names,
i sing their love of love,
i sing their throat's pain from singing so loud,
i sing the truth
 that others will try to misunderstand,
because the others, who make themselves so,
prefer this flock,
this illusion of safety,

(s)words

over freedom.

ruffling feathers
is more than your inconvenience.
it is an investment in God's sky.
in every inch of her expanse,
so that our children are not confined
to the circles you are told to march.

i will tell these fledglings
that all this sky is, was, and always will be
for them.
and that flying in formation?
that's for the birds.

public education

the armory has amnesia,
and has forgotten why it was built.
the armory has amnesia,
like it's weapons were always dull,
like it's purpose was to connect and not to cleave.
like it never filled ill-intentioned hands
with good intentions
and death.
its soldiers now soothe with gentle axes,
drive their spears with one tap a day,
say their grinding wheel is one of progress.
a knifes edge is the offered table
to rest tired elbows.
armor plated bodies
embrace dark, naked backs.
there is a blade cradling
each jawbone that does not close.
a cold steel support of every tongue
trying to remind this place of what it is.
there is a blade cradling
each jawbone that does not close.
saying
shh,
it's ok,
nobody is here to hurt you.

transfer

on a hot july morning
some kids and i had a conversation about energy.
in our vortex i chimed in
with the only absolute i had at the time:
energy cannot vanish,
and it may only be transferred into another form
or another place.

javier's eyes lit up and ballooned
like a lantern catching a meteor in its chest.
"yeah that's what i was gonna say!"
he looked at his friends
as if he confirmed the secret true,
and suddenly,
for us all,
every collision made sense.

every fireball of a gift that came to me,
opened like a rose.
every quiet (conver)sation
in the after-lunch bustle of a classroom
was now an exten(sion) cord to the sun.

we sat there, 4 monks
who skipped the ceremonies,
who caught meteors like foul balls
in between the shoddy nailing-together of essays,
all for the cause of hurling them back into play.

all in the name of transfer,
all in the name of classrooms forgotten,
these nameless powerplants
with nameless hands,

(s)words

never dying,
and ready soon for another place
deserving of their heat.

temple

public education cont.

been given a gift with this pen,
can't let anyone else tell me it was charity,
i'm writing through lies with clarity,
calling out protocols
that don't do nothin but tear at me,
procedures make disparity look like best practice,
but fuck your praxis and theories,
grant us access to realities,
the ones you hide like hide and seek,
should we count to infinity,
never look up to take a peek?
the point is to dress it up,
make grad rates like mrs. puff,
but i'm here to call their bluff,
you ask the kids if they're up to snuff?
or is in and out simply enough?
it's time to tap into potential,
see the God in every pencil,
let's burn down the factory,
it never produced for you me,
just for the high-level salaries
of people who lost what it meant
to have possibility,
and then they say that we're crazy,
that were disruptive and lazy,
but could it be that the curriculum curves
us into conformity?
that textbooks ripped out the history?
that teachers test but fail to see
that love comes before trigonometry?
that healing is home for human beings?
that we need to elevate frequency?
i got told that the american empire

(s)words

was a place dreams went to thrive,
but now i know they get born to die,
they try to tell us the bullets planted
in dark bodies were just accidents,
i heard folk say that this is "broken",
that this system was infected and cracked open,
that it was never *designed* to dash all hope and
that were all post racial and woke and
we need a 401k and the next promotion and
if you call bullshit, you've misspoken,
in blood it was wrote and
the beast had all intent to hold us by the throat and
they whisper in our ear,
tell us not to fear,
they never meant to kill,
just got broken gears,
they never meant to steal,
just gotta grease the wheels,
they never meant to lie,
this land is yours forreal,
they want you to be more than machine,
more than spokes in the wheel,
all of this is dissonance,
but i buck it and say fuck it
i need cognizance,
here's the game we play:
all this shit is by design
it's been time for us to disobey,
and these words are the way.

we are not human if we do not speak,
we are not human if we do not feel,
if we do not construct homes of solidarity
from the rubble of our own destruction.
we are not human if we cannot create,

(s)words

if we cannot incapacitate apathetic states of mind,
these black holes and restraining holds
on sublime states of growth and rhyme
are minefields we must build bridges across,
their procedures only proceed
to tame the wild growth
of seeds planted by their own misdeeds
and muffling of screams,
we are not human
if our dreams do not belong to us,
we are our stories animated,
we are the authors of life,
if only,
against any odds,
we seize our right to the pen.

job description

these contracts and signatures and accounts
decompose underfoot,
because a teacher's job description
is no less than love and our humanity
made transferrable
among roots in communication.

they whisper to me:

you are not the blood-colored blossom.
you are the thorn.

demanding blood,
as payment for any shears.

you are the thorn
enshielding the spines of the young,
reminding them of the boundless,
plated like scales along their green backs.

you rise dark and unmissable and deadly,
because their life will draw the dying near.

your job is to protect,
to keep them out of unworthy hands and vases,
and cheap plastic bouquets.

your job
is to buy them time
to find the sun.

you are the thorn

(s)words

and your day in the sun
will always be their own.

because you are them,
and they are you
forever of the same roots.

locksmith

i am the son of a locksmith.
the son of a carpenter,
whose dark fingers
were always frayed and tattered,
like the exploding ends of rope.
my dad has hands polished by fence boards and
key rings.

his shoulders sing with creaks and pops,
from swinging the hammer
and swinging open doors he put up.
he probably never considers the poetry
in being a man who literally
opens doors for others,
but i guess that's what i'm for.

and while my shoulders don't yet sing with pain,
my fingers have started to fray like his,
and i'm starting to see the poetry in that too.

i've always known i was a conduit,
always known i could see through shit,
yet we are told that in order to see it
we need the eyes that see shapes,
and not the one that sees fate.
i have heeded forked-tongue speech
and poisoned beliefs,
which speak into this titanic, galactic being,
that we can do only what we see.

but i've always known,
my dad made keys and into a key he made me.

(s)words

with these genetic ropes and their frays,
i will write words that remind
every one of my students
that rules are man-made,
and cannot govern that God-made miracle
between their ears,
that their purpose is pulsating
in the lock safes of their souls,
that this life is too short
to grow old without knowing
you did everything you could,
too short to let who you are stay misunderstood,
i want every young man who sees himself in me
to know that you are more
than what society cuts you out to be,
you are allowed to feel and to dream,
to cry and scream,
your muscles are meant to do more than break,
they are meant to move,
and create,
and uplift,
and embrace.

i want my students to know
that i will take the ropes of my father's fingers,
and take this ring of keys,
and i will help them build staircases
to the doors of their own homes.

i want them to know the sick
will tell you to stay away
and stow away what they think is wealth,
but the only thing that makes you rich in this life
is your love made useful.

(s)words

i want them to know that this home
was always theirs,
i want them to know like i did,
all you need is to inhale the air
at the top of your stairs.

your purpose is the key you cut
from the cloth you were given,
the truth your ancestors meant for you to live in,
the reason you are here is to find out why.

thanks to my pops i was given these hands,
and given a door.
and you,
young soul,
have always been the key to yours.

i know i am here to prove it.

inheritance

intermission

during the quiet parts of evening,
walking to the car, not sleeping,
those unhurried, departed,
timeless breaks
for deciding which strings to cut,
which joints to let flop,
a missing handful of seconds
is clutched to my chest,
meant only for the opera boxes
of unfocused eyes,
out of scene,
behind the obsidian of curtain.

you come to my show every night,
among the amorphous,
the smoky faces wisping in their seats,
you come to shimmer in the dust,
you come to my show every night,

even this one.

gardener

darkening earth
along the length of your fingers,
behind my ears to trickle in.
poems cannot speak what they cannot do.

you are the effect of poems.

the hoarseness in the voice
of actors who forget.

the consonants of revolution.

the woman watering flowers
in buzzing sunlight,
from a pitcher that is also her arm.

nomads

our dreams hold hands across the pillowcase,
this night.
nomadic amygdala, next.
wearing backpacks filled with torches,
winking eyes filled with horizon.
we are one dream straddling this world.
we are one step, two step, deep breath into dark
places, carving with hard feet the borderlands.
torches left in the sand
to stand in vigilance.
our dreams, my love,
nomadic.
burning.
forever pulling closer.

the exception

words are less 'this way' signs,
more fireflies in the dark.
all sounds and semantic and funny symbols
abridging this causeway.
words are like the sturdiest wiffle bats
swinging wild at the galaxies of you.
words, my love, are a small pail and plastic shovel
on all your immeasurable beaches,
gifting us all, one pail at a time,
with any of your love,
with bricks for the castle i build for you,
and will love you inside of always.

verb

love is a verb,
can't have it or hold it.

we spread seeds in our chests
intending to blanket the hillsides in each other.

our view is golden not by what is grown in shifting
sands.

our view is golden not by the intention to hold on
forever.

our view is golden
by the actions of our hands,

which hold and hold and hold.

na(ur)ture

some people enter earth already
wholly di(vine),
and no book or lecture,
or teaching or wisdom,
could make them anymore, or at all,
a vine from this unknown.
you are this garden
that has emerged from love,
under no earthly thumb.

the prophet speaking in tongues,
the shaman made abstract
in some colonizer's magazine,
they misname your magic,
unaware it's the only measurable truth in the world
amidst their violent logic and reasonable knives.
you are this ancient membrane,
photosynthesizing with God,
passing light into music,
and music into your laughter,
and your laughter into us.

by your nature,
you nurture us all.
so by nature,
we will never let you fall.

butterfly

eyelash prayers

you do this thing,
when i pluck an eyelash from your gorgeous face,
you wish on it before blowing it away,
like many do,
but when you wish on it
you hold my finger and this eyelash as if it were
scripture,
and you pray.

i have spent 4 years watching this ritual.
your scrunched-up eyebrows,
kneeling before this eyelash in reverence,
blurring the line between whimsey and
providence.

i spent 4 years wondering
how i would write this poem.
4 years pressing my ear to heaven's door,
to your chest,
hoping for the first line to this story.

but i now understand that phenomena
are forever outside of our words.

when we first met
i couldn't believe how beautiful you were,
i couldn't explain the origin of the tether
i felt between our hearts,
but i knew it was there,
like birds in free fall can't explain air,
but know it is there to catch them.

i knew when we were crammed into your twin bed

(s)words

on a saturday in november,
and you said
hey i think i—
and i said me too.

it was like faith,
or phenomena.

being with you is like catching the breath
from that laugh that puts you down,
the one that makes you snort and squeak
in between the tears,
in the aisles of rite aid, at 11:00pm
walking to target,
smashing and destroying and building houses
of ourselves in parking lots.

i have never seen the northern lights,
the aurora borealis,
but i know that
i know what it feels like.

 i can't wait to gift you bad jokes, clean dishes,
and 30-minute wrestling matches
for the rest of my life,
and i can't wait for a little audience member
or two.
i can't wait to stand on the shores
of some far-off country
and know that no matter where we dig in our feet,
there is home, a sky dancing vibrantly
in the hollow of our laced-up hands.

i can't wait to come home and feel that
nothing,

(s)words

nothing,
nothing,
is wrong.

it took me 4 years to try this poem,
because for the first time
i felt something i could not explain.

how could i translate
the only thing that makes sense in the world,
when all i've ever done is explain the things that
don't?

how can i speak the truth of this nucleus,
when the electrons are speeding
and don't intend to let me see?

maybe because we're not meant to describe it,
or to transcribe it into crude symbols.
maybe all you and i were ever meant to do
was be here and vibrate,
to be two particles on the shores of this world
destined to gravitate,
to shake, and emancipate our souls
so others can do the same.

maybe all you and i were ever meant to do
was to pluck these buzzing electrons,
these eyelashes, off each other's faces.

maybe we are only meant to pray.
to be phenomena.
to know only what it feels like.

the aurora borealis in a parking lot.

(s)words

i love you,
i love you,
i love you,

amen.

saved

at 6th and st. john

at sixth and st. john,
in san jose,
in this city tangled between worlds,
there was a fissure in the block
that showed singularity.
every sunday, this lot turned into love.
filled to the broken glass edges with food
and secondhand amps,
and toothless smiles.
i don't know who they were or why,
but i knew it was right,
watching the orangest sun
fill the fissures in these tired faces.

today, this lot is a high-rise apartment complex.

i used to talk with this houseless man,
at the 711 curb over a sandwich or black coffee.
he once asked me
what i wanted to be when i grew up.

i didn't really know,
but he looked at me, and said it immediately:
i wanted to be fishnets.

i never fully understood this until years later,
when i stared into the prefabricated metallic grin
of this high-rise, after it dragged itself over their
love.

my guess is he wanted to stretch out.
to break loaves and line.
to feed the multitudes of himself and others.

114

to take in and embrace,
for the sake of embracing a stomach,
or a heart,
or a people.

so now, as absolute as anything,
from 6th and st. john, to wherever i go,
i remember his dream,
and cast out wide.

the tallest trees

at 27 years old,
10 years past the day i became me,
i have never left this place.
never had a passport,
still don't.

back then i felt shame,
but now understand that
i was never moved by wallets or heartbeats,
because this land and her people
were always my own rhythm.

i was never meant to go
because i am magnetized to it,
by the blood in our soil.

this poem is for every young
head-reeling college type who told me
i should travel to "get new perspectives".

i believe you.
but is any perspective more real
than the one from your home's front door?

it never made sense to me
to search for myself where i am not.
maybe that is why they are always searching,
slipping, exploring, slipping,
stealing, slipping,
slipping.

someday
when my bank account gives a green light,

(s)words

i will leave to see other places
to marvel at their equally rooted hearts.
but i am so in love with this organism, this tall,
contradiction of a home,
and all of her knots and blemishes.

i now know
that the tallest trees have never moved their roots.

this poem is for every beautiful being
that plunges their hands
into the dirt outside their doors,
because nowhere else would have them,
or no way out was possible.

this poem is for the tallest trees,
whose might puts fear into saws,
whose timber will forever frame the homes
of their children.

this poem is for the ones who stayed.
for the ones who come back.
for the ones who grow tall.

for the giants
magnetized to the earth.

saved

After Miles Hodges, Bob Marley, and time

i was saved when i witnessed
another who was,

this being cut the bonds
of hands destined to love,

i was gifted these (s)words
to cut others free,

and for all my life
this cycle will repeat,

> emancipate yourselves from mental slavery,
> none but ourselves can free our minds,
> have no fear for atomic energy,
> cause none of them can stop the time.

acknowledgements

I am first a product of the incredible people around me. This book could not be in your hands without the love and support of my closet friends and family. To my incomparable parents, thank you; I will spend my life putting your love and sacrifices to good use. To my brother Lucas, #finnblood until the end; the best stuff is coming.

To my best friends, Zach, Jack, and Geremy, MP all day! To mis compadres and comadres, Jazmin, Drea, Andrea, Tina, Phil, and Kevin, thank you for being the dopest educators and fiercest colleagues. Special thanks to Phil and Kevin for proofing the book. Thanks also to an amazing artist and former student Daura Strassner for designing the cover; keep shining and creating Daura, the honor is all mine. Extra special thanks to Jazmin Hernandez; wouldn't have made this far without you compa, these lights will shine brighter every day.

To the following artists, whose art, vulnerability, and passion changed my life, thank you: Miles Hodges, Joshua Bennett, Carvens Lissaint, Alysia Harris, Saul Williams, Yasiin Bey, Bob Marley, Zack Del La Rocha, Gloria E. Anzaldúa, and Jeremy Michael Vasquez. There are dozens more, but the above folks inspired me at my lowest and fed me when I was hungriest. Your art is a blessing in this world.

To the love of my life, Julia, my beautiful, indescribable partner and my best friend: for however long we live, I don't know if I will ever be good enough with words to explain what you mean to me. Thank you for making my life full of joy and laughs. You're brilliant my love, in every way—we just getting started!

Finally, to my students, or to anyone who reads this book: remember everything you want to be in this life is already inside you. 10 years ago, I was just some kid who dreamed of great things, yet never thought them possible. Jump. With both feet. Dream more. Do more. Talk less. Time is too precious to waste. Assata said it first: you have nothing to lose but these chains.

Love always,
Finn

about the author

A.B. Finn is a poet and educator from Martinez, CA centered on the elevation, humanization, and liberation of high school-age youth. Over the last 10 years he has been equal parts athlete, student, friend, partner, and spoken word poet. His multi-dimensional identity and art are central to his practice as a teacher and healer. He teaches freshman english, creative writing, and coaches the slam poetry team at an East Contra Costa County high school. This is his first publication.

Made in the USA
San Bernardino, CA
03 December 2019